THE MALARKEY

Helen Dunmore is a poet, novelist, short story and children's writer. Her poetry books have been given the Poetry Book Society Choice and Recommendations, Cardiff International Poetry Prize, Alice Hunt Bartlett Award and Signal Poetry Award, and *Bestiary* was shortlisted for the T.S. Eliot Prize.

Her poem 'The Malarkey' won first prize in the National Poetry Competition in 2010. Her latest Bloodaxe poetry titles are *Out of the Blue: Poems 1975-2001* (2001), *Glad of These Times* (2007), and *The Malarkey* (2012).

She has published eleven novels and three books of short stories with Penguin, including *A Spell of Winter* (1995), winner of the Orange Prize for Fiction, *Talking to the Dead* (1996), *The Siege* (2001), *Mourning Ruby* (2003), *House of Orphans* (2006) and *The Betrayal* (2010), as well as a ghost story, *The Greatcoat* (2012), with Hammer. She is a Fellow of the Royal Society of Literature.

HELEN DUNMORE

The Malarkey

BLOODAXE BOOKS

ISBN: 978 1 85224 940 3

First published 2012 by
Bloodaxe Books Ltd,
Highgreen,
Tarset,
Northumberland NE48 1RP.

www.bloodaxebooks.com
For further information about Bloodaxe titles
please visit our website or write to
the above address for a catalogue.

Supported by
ARTS COUNCIL
ENGLAND

Cover design: Neil Astley & Pamela Robertson-Pearce.

Printed in Great Britain by
Bell & Bain Limited, Glasgow, Scotland.

...the most beautiful thing on this dark earth...

SAPPHO

ACKNOWLEDGEMENTS

Acknowledgements are due to the editors of the following publications where some of these poems first appeared: *The Guardian, The Independent, London Magazine, Poetry Ireland Review* and *Poetry Review*. 'The Malarkey' won first prize in the National Poetry Competition in 2010.

'I Owned a Woman Once' was commissioned by Arts Council England's website for the 2007 Bicentenary of the Abolition of the Slave Trade Act. 'Writ in Water' and 'Taken in Shadows' were first broadcast on BBC Radio 4, and '*La Recouvrance*' was first broadcast on BBC Radio 3.

CONTENTS

The Malarkey

Why did you tell them to be quiet
and sit up straight until you came back?
The malarkey would have led you to them.

You go from one parked car to another
and peer through the misted windows
before checking the registration.

Your pocket bulges. You've bought them sweets
but the mist is on the inside of the windows.
How many children are breathing?

The malarkey's over in the back of the car.
The day is over outside the windows.
No street light has come on.

You fed them cockles soused in vinegar,
you took them on the machines.
You looked away just once.

You looked away just once
as you leaned on the chip-shop counter,
and forty years were gone.

You have been telling them for ever
Stop that malarkey in the back there!
Now they have gone and done it.
Is that mist, or water with breath in it?

Come Out Now

Come out now and stand beside me,
grasp the rail as the swell lifts you
above this inky, innocent city

which has put away all but the whoop of an ambulance
quickly suppressed, all but the chain of lights
slung westward across the Mendips,

all but the last cry of a drunk by the docks,
the salt taste of a locked-out tide,
the clipping hooves of a police horse.

Come out now and stand beside me.
I promise I won't look
and won't breathe in too deeply

the first smoke from the cigarette
you have naturally lit.

Here are only things you love.
Look to your left, where the *Matthew*
rears its cargo of flags,

or where masts chink in the dark
and a rat pours down a rope
from bollard to boat.

Come out now and stand beside me,
look at the swans asleep,
tell me gossip about Keats,

drink your drink and smoke your cigarette,
let me ask you all those questions
or perhaps ask nothing.

The gulls say dawn is coming
but I believe that they are wrong
and the dark goes on for ever,

so come out now and stand here
in shirtsleeves although it's midwinter
quietly regarding water and stars.

The Inbox

It is the same electrical impulse as ever.
Look at the dates now: more than ten years
since that first empty message,

which was only your Hotmail address
blinking its way to my inbox
in slow, careful triumph

and with a touch of shyness: was this you, really,
using voice-recognition software
with such wary aplomb?

And then email after email went AWOL
and neither of us could work it out
until: *Yes, this time I got your brief note*

saying you had tried and tried, God knows
where the previous emails went
but now we're in business.

You tried to access the Kremlin webcam
to catch a glimpse of me there,
emailed my daughter to say how glad you were

that you did not have to learn Swedish
in order to enjoy Shakespeare.
Sometimes the software failed. *Lovelypage!*

you typed, *Didn't know of it before your email*
forgive brevity but my via-Voice is dumb.
I told you that crashing was all too common

and when the software worked, you wrote:
This celebrates the return
of your dictator father.

How far, how very far from that
you ever were.

Boatman

Give me that red tub like a child's drawing
give me the catamaran
or the ferry zig-zagging

give me any or all of them
and meanwhile hold tight to my hand
for the water is wide where we stand.

The water is wide where we stand
and we are weary with waiting
but the boatman will not come.

I gave you coins to hold ready
but it must have been then
that I looked away from the water

and the boat came and went
as you held on valiantly
with your small change for Charon.

We are cold and weary with waiting.
You say there is no boatman
there was never any boatman

and I say, hold tight to my hand
for the water is wide where we stand.

I Owned a Woman Once

so glossy-fleshed, so high-coloured
my blood swept in my veins
she was rich and heaped in the belly
as the Bible says
she was fertile as the bank of a river
when the flood falls and the mud makes food,

I clothed her as I wanted to clothe her
I housed her as I wanted to house her
I put food on her plate to fatten her,

I owned a woman once so high-coloured
so dark and rich in the eyes
my blood would not be still in my veins
my eyes would not stop watching her –
a callous on her heel made my belly quiver –

I put food on her plate to fatten her
I put oil on her hair
she was fertile as the bank of a river,

I owned a woman once so high-coloured
so slow and sure in her walk
that all eyes walked with her,
I owned her from broken toenail
to breath that misted my mirror

and I clothed her as I wanted to clothe her,
her flesh hidden, her body shrouded
while she fattened with my child,

yes, mostly it was sweet to own her
but sometimes I had to punish her
for her eyes everywhere looking
for all the moist folds of her body hidden
and the rich darkness of her eyes looking.

Soon it came to her time
and this woman I owed lay on the ground
in the room I kept for her
with the midwife I paid for her
but her belly would not release the child

and the cage of her hips would not let go the child.
The midwife said she came to it too young
maybe, this woman I owned

but believe me
she was straight out of the Bible
so glossy-fleshed, so high-coloured
so heaped and rich in the belly
with one bare callous on her heel.

When I should be working
on one of those afternoons
where the lights come on early
and rain spatters the windows
I take down an anthology
with a design of blue snowflakes
over the purple ground –
Longman English Series, Poetry
1900 to 1965
published (cased) in 1967.

T.S. Eliot looks desperate
in front of a BBC microphone
the size of a parking meter
and Thom Gunn's as glamorous
as his own sad captains.
In the margins, my husband's
young unreadable handwriting –
out of it springs a line,
a pulse of thought
he had years before we met.

In *Notes*, Lawrence is mildly taken to task
for the way his repetitions can degenerate,
though warmly praised for 'Gentians'.
I remember the teacher's voice
as we dug our heels into the flanks
of *Sons and Lovers*, on the home straight
or so we thought,
Does anyone know what he's on about?
Helen? But in Longman's Elysian
field the poems only answer
and the poets only ask.

Writ in Water

They make him a plaster saint of poetry, with his eyes turned up to heaven. But it wasn't like that.

Winter. Rome at last. The terrible voyage from England was done. We'd found lodgings and a doctor. All he had to do was to get well.

By day the noise of the fountain was almost hidden. There were women selling chickens and fresh milk, children playing, pails clattering, the creak of wheels and the clop of horses' hooves. We used to count the different sounds, and he always won. But at night the fountain played clearly. Bernini's fountain, with its fantastic coils of marble and gushing water.

'Our Roman water is pure, not like the filthy water in Napoli,' said our landlady, with a toss of her head. Signora Angeletti was slippery with the truth, but she was right about the water. I made sure there was always a full pitcher by his bed. Fever made him thirsty.

They've burned everything in our lodgings. The table we ate off, the bed he lay in. Even the shutters that I swung open at dawn so that he could gaze down the steps to the piazza and the life of a new day. They stripped our rooms. It's the law here. The Roman authorities are terrified of consumption.

'Please move aside, Signor Severn. We have our duty to perform.'

But the ceiling remains, the one he lay under. They couldn't take away those flowers he gazed at every day until he died. Sometimes he thought he was already in his grave, with flowers growing over him. He dreamed of water bubbling out of the earth, and violets in damp, sweet grass.

'You should be painting, Severn. Why are you not painting?'

When we first came, when he was strong enough, he would sit in the winter sun and watch the artists in the piazza.

'You have more talent than any of them, Severn.'

I still have this little sketch of him: see. There were others but they've been lost. Maybe someone has taken them, I don't know.

When you draw something, you never forget it. It was night, and there was one candle burning. That was enough light to draw by. It was a still, mild night, even though it was only February. But Spring comes early in Rome. It was the last night of his life.

The flame of the candle barely moved. The fountain was loud. He was asleep, cast up on the pillow like a shipwrecked man. His hair was stuck to his forehead with sweat.

I shall never forget that night. He'd tried to prepare me. Warn me.

'Have you ever seen anyone die, Severn? I have. I nursed my brother Tom.'

Sometimes, after a fit of coughing, he would lie so still that I thought he was already dead.

'I must warn you, Severn, if you persist in nursing me you'll see nothing of Rome but a sickbed and a sick man. Believe me, it's better to give me the laudanum.'

There was a full bottle of laudanum. I gave it to him drop by drop, as Doctor Clarke ordered.

'Give me all of it, Severn. You don't understand what it is to die as I am going to die.'

But how could I allow him to destroy his immortal soul? I did not trust myself. I gave the laudanum to Dr Clarke, for fear I'd weaken.

He asked me to go the cemetery. He wanted me to describe the place where he was to lie. I told him about the goats cropping the grass, the young shepherd guarding his flock, the daisies and violets that grew so thickly over the graves.

'It's very quiet,' I told him. 'You can hear the breeze blowing through the grass. There's a pyramid which marks an ancient tomb.'

He lay back and closed his eyes. After a while he asked me whose tomb it was.

'I enquired,' I told him. 'His name was Caius Cestius, and he was a great man of the first century.'

'A great man... A very rich man at least, my dear Severn, if he had a pyramid built for his tomb. Is it large?'

'Large enough.'

'Does it cast a shadow?'

'I suppose so.'

His cough caught at him. I propped him with pillows.

'You should not talk,' I told him. He moved his head from side to side, restlessly. Then he said,

'You must understand that I will not regain my health now, Severn. I have studied enough anatomy to know that.'

We lived in our own world all those weeks. The next cup of broth, the next visit from Dr Clarke, the beating-up of pillows, the lighting of fires and measuring of medicines. Some days I hadn't a moment to call my own. Some nights I did not undress.

I was glad of it. He lay with the marble egg given to him by Miss Brawne in his hand. Women keep such an egg by them when they sew, to cool their fingers. He held that marble hour after hour, day after day. It soothed him as nothing else did. He wanted to know why he was still living, when everything was finished for him. This posthumous life, he called it.

He was sorry after he said it.

'My poor Severn, you have enough to do without listening to my misery.'

We had a piano carried upstairs so that I could play for him. He loved Haydn.

'Don't you hear that they are the same, Severn: the piano, and the fountain? Listen. But what am I thinking of? You cannot listen to yourself play, any more than a blackbird can hear itself sing.'

I was there as the days wore him down. His other friends, Dilke and Brown and Reynolds and the rest, they were far away in England. Now we fight over his memory like cats.

But it was to me that he spoke. I wiped the sweat off his face and washed him and changed his linen. I told him about the sheep that roamed over the graves. He smiled. He never tired of the sheep, the goats, the shepherd boy and the violets. The next day he would ask again, as if he'd already forgotten.

But I don't think he forgot. Words were like notes of music to him. He liked to hear how they fell.

'Sometimes I think I am already buried, with flowers growing over me,' he said, as he stared up at the ceiling where the painted flowers swarmed.

Signora Angeletti became suspicious. She waylaid the doctor, asking what was wrong. Was it consumption?

'I am a charitable woman, but I must think of my other lodgers.'

I didn't know the laws of Rome then. She feared that they would strip her rooms and burn everything. I suppose she was right, but she was compensated. She lost nothing.

I heard the patter of Signora Angeletti's voice from the mezzanine. We were in her hands. No other boarding-house would take us now: he was too obviously ill.

He understood Signora Angeletti very well. She gave us a bad dinner, not long after we came, and he threw it straight out of the window onto the Steps. A crowd of urchins came from nowhere and scrabbled for it.

'She won't serve us such stuff again,' he said, and he was right. She had given us rubbish, to see if we were willing to swallow it. I wished I had his firmness. I was nervous with Signora Angeletti, and she knew it. In those ways he was more worldly than I was.

Yes, they make him a plaster saint of poetry, with his eyes turned up to heaven. They fight over his memory, shaping it this way and that. But I remember how he rocked with laughter when that dinner splattered on the marble steps!

'My best plate!' screamed Signora Angeletti. But he said,

'If that plate is the best you have, Signora, then I am very sorry for you.'

After that the dinners were always hot and good.

I've told the story of those months so many times that they hardly seem to belong to me. If I say that they were the high point of my life, you will misunderstand me. You may even accuse me of cruelty. A man lay dying, and I say it was the high point of my existence? How can I recall those months of agony and dwindling hope, except with a shudder?

I remember the nights chiefly. We set the candles so that as one died, the next one would light from its burning thread. Once he said that there was a fairy lamplighter in the room. The flame would burn down until it seemed about to collapse on itself. He watched intently all the while. When the next sprang up and began to bloom, he would allow himself to close his eyes.

When I was very tired the room seemed to sway and the noise of the fountain reminded me of our voyage from England. Sometimes I fell asleep for a few seconds and really believed that I felt the motion of the ship under me.

I remember one incident which I have never written down, or spoken of even. I was in the small room which was intended for my studio. I thought of his words.

'You should be painting, Severn! Here you are in Rome and you do not paint at all.'

I was standing at the table, going through my sketchbook. It contained a few studies which I hoped might be worth further work. I had sketched the cemetery for him. The pyramid of Caius Cestius, with the young shepherd sitting on the grass. But I had never shown him the sketch. How can a man say to another:

'Look, here is the place where you will be buried. Just there, where that shepherd sits and dreams.'

I decided to be buried there too, beside him. My heart grew easier then. I felt no more estrangement from him.

As I turned the pages of my sketchbook, a cruel truth hit me like a blow. The reason I could not paint was not so much my cares for the invalid, as my fear that I would never paint well enough. Here I was in Rome, the heart of the painted world. Here were my masters all around me. Nothing I achieved could ever equal one of Bernini's marble coils.

The noise of the fountain grew louder. It was drowning me. It told to give up, stop pretending that there was merit in my pitiful daubs or in the travelling scholarship I'd been so proud to win. Rome would wash me away, as it had washed away a thousand others, leaving no trace. I seized hold of the leaves of my sketchbook, meaning to rip them out so that no one would ever guess the contemptible folly of my ambitions.

At that moment I felt a touch on my shoulder. A clasp, a warm, wordless, brotherly clasp. The fingers gripped my shoulder and then shook it a little, consolingly, encouragingly.

I knew straightaway that it was him. God knows how he had dragged himself out of that bed and come to find me. I could not imagine how he'd guessed at my anguish. I said nothing. His clasp was enough. After a moment the grip of the hand tightened, and then left me.

He was going back to bed, I thought. But there were no retreating footsteps. I looked over my shoulder. No one was there. He could not possibly have moved so fast. I hurried to the bedroom and there he was, deeply asleep. I stared at his face and I knew that he was dying, not weeks or months in the future, but now. How had I not recognised it before?

I sat down by the bed. My sketchbook was still in my hand. I got up again, noiselessly, and fetched what I needed from the little room. I was ready to draw him now.

The noise of the fountain. The sound of a pencil moving. His breath. A long, dragging pause. Another breath. You can live an entire life between one breath and the next. That's where my life was spent, in one night, in one room. The rest is memory.

Dis

The obvious story, my darling,
is that Dis caught you
into his dark kingdom.

I don't know where I was
when he seared the grass
with winter footprints.

If your mother was not there
whose hand could hold you
when he opened the earth for you?

I see your fingers
twist in your lap
as you keep mute.

You will not eat the seeds.
You know what he offers you.
They glow softly, like coral

in the blue vaults of this hell
where I am only a shadow
squeaking its anguish.

Let me take your place in the dark.
Dis knows you have eaten nothing
of his gifts, his pomegranates.

For months he's kept you,
whispering 'Your mother
never loved you as I love you.'

Part your hands, my darling.
Let me pour into them
salt and grain.

Newgate

Beneath the bulk of the block the bins
sweat with a week's refuse.
In the concrete corridor lines of lockers
gape, hiding a man who's

back-to-the-wall, intent
as the last words of his sentence
lock together, his own jigsaw
starting to make sense.

He tunes up a stifle of terror
in the girl he's got by the throat
while she claws at his fingers.
He's bored. He flicks the remote.

He's had enough of all this noise
and endless interference –
lights going out, pupils pinpoints.
Why can't they let him be as he is?

Far away a bin lid drops down
and the arches of Newgate tighten
as dead men walk through them
on the way to their dying.

What architect first squinnied
to fix this perspective? Getting it right
meant waiting for the reaction
when it came into sight.

Now they are breathing. Now
guards shovel the quicklime.
Now the girl uncurls from her sofa,
and takes the rubbish down.

The guards whistle, nonchalant
as the prison van backs up.
Even now the soiled dark of the cell
even now the thrash of the girl.

At Ease

When I was four at the feet
of my grandpa and my great-uncle
we heard how well Frank had done

all those years with his war pension.
He got the better of them.
They doled it when he was young

mustard-gassed and not likely to live
long enough to do more than dint it –
but he married on it.

That was in the Great War
when my grandpa kept order
in the burning Dardanelles.

You wouldn't guess how many flowers
grew in those brown hills.
For a month they bled anemones

then they were blue with hyacinths –
little wild ones, not like these.

Harbinger

Small, polished shield-bearer
abacus of early days
and harbinger of life's happiness

that the world offers
things scarlet and spotted
to alight, hasping and unhasping
unlikely wings,

that there can be three or thousands
but not a plague of ladybirds
no, a benediction of ladybirds
to enamel the weeds.

Small, polished shield-bearer
abacus of early days,
harbinger of life's happiness.

The Hyacinths

Pressed in the soil's black web, nursed by the rough
offhand embrace of frost, the hyacinths
turn in their sleep. Such blunt stabbings
against the paperiness of ancient skin,
such cell-memory, igniting
a slow fuse laid in the ground.

Pressed in the soil's black web, rocked back to sleep
by the storm that tugs at the holly tree's roots
the hyacinths know they are listening
to the west wind that kills them,
but they are safe, having given themselves to darkness.
All they desire is not to flower.

Hyacinths, when I see you forced from the soil
glossy and over-talkative
with your loud scent and demand for attention
I will put you back to sleep, forking
the long-fibred darkness over you.

The Night Workers

All you who are awake in the dark of the night,
all you companions of the one lit window
in the knuckled-down row of sleeping houses,

all you who think nothing of the midnight hour
but by three or four have done your work
and are on the way home, stopping

at traffic lights, even though there is no one
but you in either direction. How different the dark is
when day is coming; you know all this.

All you who have kept awake through the dark of the night
and now go homeward; you, charged with the hospital's
vending-machine coffee; you working all night at Tesco,

you cleaners and night-club toilet attendants,
all you wearily waiting for buses
driven by more of you, men who paint lines

in the quiet of night, women with babies
roused out of their sleep so often
they've given up and stand by their windows

watching the fog of pure neon
weaken at the rainy dawn's coming.

Agapanthus above Porthmeor

(for Patrick and Alexa)

Blue against blue; blue into deeper blue.
Skeins of light at the horizon
and the flower here, touchable,
a blue that gathers to it
the sky, the sea.

Tender, exotic,
the agapanthus was not born here
but it belongs here
with its own essence of blue
echoing the sea's deep stripes.

You pause on the hill, breathless
and look back at the silk of the horizon
at the wide miles you have climbed
to be together, here
and wanting nothing.

Blue against blue, blue into deeper blue.
This is the day of the agapanthus,
of flower-filled sureness.
Love is here, touchable,
gathering our lives to it.

Visible and Invisible

(for Jane)

That dream when we were young,
that hunt for the magic
which might make it happen:
invisibility.

Such glittering cloaks
such eagerly swallowed
rose-petal potions

but we stayed solid and sunlit
jumping on our own shadows
defeated by ourselves.

We didn't know how easy
the trick would turn out to be.
All you do is let the years pass

and quietly on its own it happens.
You only have to let the airy cloak of years
fall on your shoulders.

The Snowfield

No matter how wide the snowfield
you don't walk in your own footprints –
each day the apparent freedom
narrows, sun greases
your steps to ice

until the steep track glistens beneath you
and you dare not go on
but stand trembling
bruised, struggling to balance,

you stand trembling as night comes on
on the wicked lip of the hill that stands
between you and home.

Lemon tree in November

(for Kurt and Caroline Jackson)

Dark, present, scattering night,
the blows of the wind
on the upturned hull of home

the stub of the lighthouse wiped out
the land crouched

our lemon tree
shaking its leaves
in the wet garden

the palm at the window
hissing, rattling

as the lighthouse beam
buds and grows
on a gnarl of foam.

Dark, present, scattering night
with the curtains bulging
and the wind again
on the upturned hull of home.

Bildad

The dark, present, scattering night,
the thick stub of the light-house folded
and put away like linen
but still the bud of its light opening
over a gnarl of foam,

such an oncoming
dark in the garden
the slim leaves of the lemon tree
quite gone,
its structure hung
by the light of its fruit.

Palm leaves hiss
in the rough hands of the wind,
that wind again
kneading the air as it wants –
The more the decades
the less we belong,
tangential as thistle
while the wind booms

seizing the chimneys
lifting the curl
of our ill-made sunroof.
Untouchable
the wind does what it wants
playing harmonica
on the upturned hull of home:

such quaintness
to build a house here,
to slip a bribe to the rock
not to open under it
and pay the sea to turn back.

Tonight the ravaging of cliffs
is the hunger of pack-animals
jostling for place,
hunting the man named Job
in the land of Uz

whose imagination painted him
a righteous kingdom
where he washed his steps with butter.
But the wind answered him
and *naked*, Job said, *I came
and naked will return*
as he sat on the ground.

The wind scours our faces with stars.
We wriggle like children
eyes screwed up tight,
our quaint imaginations
busy planting lemons
lulled by the ear-drowse
and zing of bees.

There is a cup, blue, full to the brim
with tea. There is catnip
and the brief shade of an olive tree.
Outside, a dusty road, and from time to time
walkers, who greet each other with silence
or a curt nod which affirms
the rubric of the stranger
and we are all strangers here.

At the far side of the earth's curve
waiting to flood our habitations
there is always the night
borne on a wind beyond imagination
and not to be troubled with,
a wind that chases its load of stars
like dust beneath the broom,

There is the dark, present, scattering night,
the thick stub of the light-house folded
and put away like linen,
the bud of its light blocked
by the bulk of a new roof.

Bildad said: *how can he be clean*
that is born of a woman?
And so answers a mob of men
hunting down a girl
with a wind of sticks and stones
as they strip her and beat her
from town to town
assisted by bicycles
and mobile phones.

I trouble myself with the snipping of catnip.
If I sit on the ground
it will comfort no one
and rake no spittle from the wind.

Skulking

A heap of cloud
skulks over the roofs
like the summit of a bully's ambition –

the short dark days of winter
dear to me
as a bully to his mother.

Basement at Eighteen Folgate Street

I know them by their shoes –
clean kid on a Sunday,
work-boots on Mondays
chipping sparks from the pavement,
or skittery dance shoes
going to the Palais on a Saturday –
the cuff-cuff-cuff of too many lives –

Barclays Bank, St Ives

Old men with sticks and courteous greeting
who have learned the goodness of days
and give freely the hours it takes
to reach the fathomless depth of the pipe's tamped bowl
or the corolla of that daffodil
damply unfolding, or a toothless smile from a pushchair
that irradiates the granite morning.

One of them puts out a finger
dark with work and nicotine
to touch the blooming cheek of a great-granddaughter.
How close they are to the rim of the earth
while the cashpoint zizzes out figures
and the young go up and down the street with backpacks,
their eyes justified and full of purpose.

Playing Her Pieces

(for Thomas Hardy in 1912)

He takes the temperature of his heart.
O feverish instrument that played so crazily
with such wild fingers and still struck
dead on the note,

is it cool yet? Does it stand apart
like a man civilly bowing a woman
whom he no longer loves
through a door he will not enter?

O feverish instrument of art,
he kneels beside the body of his love
to wash his hands between her ribs
where the blood throbbed.

Look at her playing her pieces. Start
her song again, the one that wearied him
as her dull flesh wearied him, her stiff
intransigent difficultness –

all of it laved now. Let his fingers part
as her soul slips through them –
O feverish instrument, let
the man sit and write.

Pianist, 103,

looks at the morning
where she will play
from nine to one
and says how beautiful
each note, each sun.

Such scales of suffering –
no one can weigh them,
she says how beautiful
each smile, each footfall
each startled face
in the heat of love –

The Torn Ship

In what torn ship soever I embark
That ship shall be my emblem of Thy ark...

JOHN DONNE,
'A Hymn to Christ, at the Author's Last Going into Germany'

I was up and watching
that night the torn ship rode
through the lock gates and so came on –

In the guise of midnight
it slowly glided
owl-like in stubborn purpose
broken by the hands of the storm.

So it came on
blackly on the black water,
pulse by pulse it found harbour –
Through the shut lock gates it melted

to the ring and rocking
of a hundred tall masts
and then the swans woke from their nest
and stood unfurling

their steeple wings in warning
as the shade and shadow passed
of whatsoever torn ship it was.
Remember this was no ark

but something broken
long before the dark took it down.

Taken in Shadows

Beautiful John Donne. Who wouldn't want you? You lean slightly forward, arms folded over your body as if to protect it from all the women who might otherwise tear off your clothes.

And yet, now that I look closely – and I do look very, very closely, John – there's a teasing touch of something I can only call ... *readiness...* in the way you're sitting for your portrait. Take your eyes. They are clear hazel, brooding on something that is beyond me and a little to my right. What has caught your gaze? How many generations of women – and men too, I'm sure, men too – must have longed to make you turn to them. But your gaze has never shifted. Not once, in over four centuries.

Your mouth is red. The shadow of your moustache – so dandyish, so eloquently shaved into points! – serves to emphasise the perfect cut of your upper lip. Your lower lip is full, sensuous. Red lips, hazel eyes, arched, dark eyebrows. Your jaw is a line of perfection. The shadow of your broad-brimmed hat can't hide the modelling of your temples. Your long fingers rest on your sleeve's rich satin. You gleam in light from a source which is forever invisible, outside the frame. And then there's the fall of your collar, the exquisiteness of lace thrown over darkness.

You're in your glory. From where you sit inside your portrait, it's the present day. The present moment, even, and you're caught in it. Your right ankle itches, but you suppress the urge to scratch. Your heart throbs with its own quick life. Soon the sitting will be over, but you don't mind the time you spend here. The artist is anonymous to me, but not to you. You know him well. This portrait is important to you and you'll keep it with you all your life.

The moment I look away, you smile, stand up and stretch like a cat. The artist, of course, has taken careful note of your pose before it dissolves.

'Until next time,' he says, wiping a brush.

'Until next time,' you agree.

You've given me the slip again, John. You're back in your own world. It's 1595, a date which I know well. I've studied your period, and I dress you in my rags of knowledge. I can analyse your social status in the light of your lace collar. You are history, John. You wouldn't like that, I know. The fact that I can speak and you cannot would seem quite wrong to you, given the relative values of what we have to say.

You know 1595 from the inside, by the touch of satin, the warmth of a spring day, the gamey smell of your own body, the bite of a flea at the nape of your neck. For you, the door is about to open into a stream of May sunshine that will make you blink. For me, it has closed forever.

The Elizabethan age has eight more years to run. The old Queen has kept the show on the road so much longer and more brilliantly than anyone had a right to expect. She has united the country. Those who are not united are dead, imprisoned, exiled, silenced or lying very low indeed.

You're in your glory, but also in those shadows that wrap themselves around you like a cloak. Your mother has gone into exile, and your brother died in Newgate two years ago, because he harboured a priest. Your fellow Catholics are food for the scaffold. That is what hanging, drawing and quartering is all about. It does so much more than kill: it turns a protesting soul into blood-slimed joints of meat, laid on the block for the public appetite.

You don't yet know for sure that England will not return to the faith, not soon, not ever, but I should say that you've already made an educated guess. You have, as we know, a great deal of imagination. You will do nothing which will allow your body to be seized, racked, beaten, imprisoned, to die in its own shit and blood and vomit on the clammy ground. You will not be carted to Tyburn to be pelted with the crowd's insults, spittle and rotten fruit before you are lynched. Nor are you willing to endure the long, dismal martyrdom of being jobless, without influence, friends or position, bled dry by penal taxes. You are already preparing to leave the home of your soul, and find another if you can.

I look at your long, slender fingers. Perhaps you played upon the lute, as well as upon the emotions of a hundred women. Beautiful, beautiful John Donne. How were you to know that there'd be generations snuffling greedily over your portrait? You couldn't guess, any more than Sylvia Plath guessed what would happen to her image after the lens clicked, her radiant smile faded and she got up from where she'd been sitting on a bank of daffodils with her infant son in her arms. How could you estimate the wolfish hunger of a public not yet born?

You and Sylvia are the kind we really love. You make us feel that we can climb right inside your lives. The only frustrating thing is that you keep looking at things we cannot see. You will never meet our eyes.

Listen, John, I can tell you what's going to happen to you after you take off that lace collar. You're going to screw up on a royal scale. You'll fall in love with the wrong girl, mis-calculate about her father coming round to your secret marriage (he won't, not for years). You'll find yourself in a cottage full of children, most of whom have coughs or colds or sweating sickness or some other early seventeenth-century malady, for much of the time. Life will become an everlasting winter, smelling of herbs, baby shit, sour milk and dirty clothes.

John Donne
Anne Donne
Undone

I wonder what your wife thought when she read that little epigram? Some of your children will die, or be born dead. With any luck you won't feel it as we would these days. Poor little rabbits, you'll be sorry enough for them while they're alive, screaming their heads off, wanting all the things that nobody's able to give them, such as antibiotics, central heating and a trip to Disneyland.

I expect your wife will have to sell that lace collar to pay for one of her confinements. You'll lose your job. Everyone who owes you a grudge will take the chance to kick you now that you're down. You'll be out of favour for years. For all the effort you've put into avoiding martyrdom, you'll achieve your own not very glorious exile in a borrowed cottage in Mitcham.

But none of that has happened yet.

'Come and look,' says the artist, and you saunter round to his side of the easel. Next week he will begin to paint your hands. It has already been decided that you will wear no rings. You don't need to trumpet your status or your prospects, and besides, the artist prefers not to mar the effect of your long, eloquent fingers.

You stare thoughtfully at your unfinished portrait. It will wreak havoc for generations, that painted face. Cohorts of fifteen-year-old girls will fall for you and feel for you, as you struggle in the swamp of domesticity. *'His wife had a baby a year, isn't that gross? She must of been pregnant, like, all the time.'*

But your true lovers are more sensitive. We know the inside story. You were undone indeed, you and Anne. A piece of her soul went awry when she married you, and a piece of your soul left your body to meet it. You were never intact again. You tried to write with the noise of your little ones ringing in your ears. You went upstairs, you went downstairs, you went up to town and down to the country, you went to my lady's chamber but there they still were, babbling, squabbling, screaming and squawking, catching quinsies and spotted fevers and scarlet fevers and marsh fevers.

You had no money and each child cost so much. Months of sickness and weariness for Anne, heavy clambering of the stairs, dull aches that heralded the rack of labour. The children's voices floated, skirling. Tom fought with John, Constance bossed little Mary.

Mary died. Baby Nicholas died. The stillborn unnamed baby died. They floated off, little eager vagrant souls who had found flesh, but not for quite long enough. They were turned out of their bodies like tenants who hadn't paid the rent. They left fragments of themselves: their blind, eager sucking, the drum of their feet inside the womb. Mary's first words drifted around your house like feathers.

I was one of those fifteen-year-olds, of course, and head-over-heels in love with you. You were so unhappy. With what brave grace you wrote of your 'hospital at Mitcham' where the children grew and the poems shrank. You were kept busy writing begging letters. You had to have patrons, even though so many had turned their backs. No one wants to be contaminated by social failure. You'd stepped out so boldly and now you had to fight for a foothold somewhere, anywhere.

I would have done anything for you, when I was fifteen. I even made friends with your wife. Yes, in that hasty, obsequious way of a very determined girl when she pits herself against a grown woman and a mother. I could babysit for Anne perhaps. Surely she would like to have a nice sit down? I shepherded little Constance and John and Tom and Mary into the other room, sang sweetly to them, gave them their dinner and washed their bare, rosy feet. A curl of green snot crawled in and out of Mary's nostril as she breathed. I found a rag and wiped it away tenderly.

There was silence from the bedroom. Anne must be sleeping, I thought, and no wonder. Her pregnancy looked like a growth on her skinny body. Her skin was blue-white. She wore a married woman's cap and the hair that escaped from it was thin and lustreless.

I wonder, by my troth, what thou and I
Did til we loved?

48

Let Anne sleep for a while, poor thing. I didn't want the children to wake her, so I hoisted Mary onto my knee and began to tell a story. She twisted round in my lap and pressed my lips together with her fingers. The others pinched and poked and whinged. I couldn't even come up with a nursery rhyme. It was time to wake Anne up again.

I tiptoed to the door of her bedroom. Your bedroom too, but I prefer not to think about that. I heard something I didn't expect: laughter. A slash of dread went through me. You'd got in there somehow. You were laughing with her, privately. But no. I peeped through the gap in the door and there she was, quite alone, sitting up in bed and reading. A few seconds later she laughed again, and looked up with vague shining eyes as if she expected someone. She didn't see me, of course.

I've put a stop to all that sort of thing. I'm not fifteen any more. The past is the past and it's better, much better for everyone, if it doesn't come alive. I don't want to see your beautiful face grow old. I don't want to see your wife's plain, worn features light up when she thinks I might be you, ready to share her laughter. I went too far that time, but I've pulled myself back and I'm in command again. You are history, John. You've written all your poems. Your tongue is still. I refuse to be coerced into seeing things your way.

You're back inside the portrait frame, beautiful and contained. Your red lips. Your high cheekbones and the pure almond cut of your eyelids. It's no surprise that you liked this portrait so much. What a blend of sexual magnetism and intellectual glamour. But I've just noticed something else that I've never seen before. There's a glint of humour in your eyes, as if you're wondering how many more centuries of devastation you'll be capable of before your painted magic fades. There are just the two of us, John. Why won't you look at me? Why won't you tell me what you see?

Prince Felipe Prospero

(1657-1661)

He wears a silver bell
so that in the shadow
of palace corridors
he can always be followed,

he wears a ball of amber
to ward off infection,
he wears an amulet
against malediction,

so blessed and protected
with hair like thistledown
and a gaze the painter
'found in heaven'.

He wears the slightest of frowns
but keeps to his station
as we do, watching him.

Picture Messages

of trees: olive and lemon,
of eggs and bacon
of my father at The Tin Drum
on his last weekend
smiling,
with coffee in front of him.

We went to Latinos
to eat *gambas a la plancha*
while you chatted to Mariella,
we went home and you sat
in the red armchair.
Your hand took mine:
it was that half hour before departing.

You took my bag to the door
and had your hand on the lift button
as usual pretending surprise
that anyone could shun
the judder of that contraption
with its random halts between floors,

I said I would see you soon
after a last embrace,
and you kept your hand raised
until I was swallowed
in the dark of the turning staircase.

Lethe

Is it Lethe or is it dock water?
Either has the power.

The neighbourhood killer
is somewhere quietly washing up

dipping and dipping his fork
in the dirty water.

The police vans sit crooning
on the crux of the Downs.

How quickly the young girls walk
from work and from the shops.

The frost that was bone cold
has eased into rain, the dock water

takes everything and turns it brown.

The Queue's Essentially

The queue's essentially
docile surges get us
very slowly somewhere.

Like campfire, life springs up –
that pair ahead of me
(newly landed on Easyjet, he
shunts the wheeled, packed
tartan suitcase
inch by inch

through jumpy fractures of brake-light
on wet pavement) –

that pair ahead of me
who graze on their vegetable pasty
and pass it in Polish
from his hand to hers –

so intimate, rained-upon –
learning so quickly it will be a mistake
to take that taxi
all the way to Kilburn –

The Captainess of Laundry

I am the captainess of laundry
and I sing to its brave tune,
to the crack and the whip and the flap of the sheets
and the rack going up, going down, going down
and the rack going up and going down,

I am the captainess of laundry
and I salt my speech with a song
of the bleach and the blue and the colours holding true
and the glaze of the starch on my skin, my skin,
and the glaze of starch on my skin,

I am the captainess of laundry
and I swing my basket through the town
with the sheets and the shirts and the white petticoats
and a snowy-breasted cover tied around, tied around
and a snowy-breasted cover tied around.

The Day's Umbrellas

On the same posts each evening
the harbour cormorants
hang out their wings to dry
like the day's umbrellas
as the late ferry passes.

In sour-sweet ramparts of ivy
the blackbirds call
drowsily, piercingly.
Above them the gulls
are casing the terraces.

Thickly, the pigeons
groom their own voices
as parents in the half-light
tiptoe away from babies
over their heads in sleep.

The Deciphering

How busy we are with the dead in their infancy,
who are still damp with the sweat of their passing,
whose hair falls back to reveal a scar.

We think of wiping their skin, attending them
in the old way, but are timid, ignorant.
We walk from the high table where they are laid

leaving their flesh royally mounded
just as they have left it
for the undertakers to cherish.

We consider the last kiss,
the taste and the grain of it.
The lift doors squeeze open, then shut.

All day we think that we have lost our car keys.
There is a feeling in the back of the mind
as we eat a meal out on the balcony

but the door refuses to open
and although my sisters have prepared food elaborately
you do not advance to us, smiling.

The children have put sauce on the side of their plates
thinking you will come and swipe a chip,
thinking this meal is one you cooked

as always, humming to yourself in the kitchen,
breaking off to tap the barometer
and watch starlings roost on the pier.

How long it takes to stop being busy with that day,
each second of it like the shard
of a pot which someone has laboured to dig up

and piece together without knowledge
of language or context.
Slow, slow, the deciphering.

The Tarn

Still as the water is
the wind draws on it in iron

this is the purple country, the border
where we threw ourselves down
onto the heather.

Even the lapwing knows how to pretend.
She runs with her broken wing
to hide the fact of her young.

A cold small rain spatters the tarn
the wind writes on the dark water.

The Gift

You never wanted the taste
of the future on your tongue.
How often, hurriedly, I saw you
swallow a premonition.

If the gift comes, you told me,
do not let it in.
Obedient, I wrote poems
but the gift still came

though the doors were bolted.
I'm here, it told me
to make you know things
but not their names.

What Will You Say

(after Baudelaire)

What will you say, my soul, poor and alone,
and my heart with its heart sucked out,
What will you say tonight to *the one*
(if she's really the one this time)?

totheverybeautifultotheverygoodtotheverydear
Ah no. Speak clearly. What will you say
to her, so good, so fair, so dear
whose heavenly gaze has made your desert flower?

You'll say you've had enough. No more.
You've no pride left but what goes to praise her.
No strength left but in her douce power,
no senses but what she gives.

Sweet authority! Douce power!
or do you mean you're shit-scared
to go anywhere without her?
Is she your mother?

Her look clothes us in light.
Her ghost is the scent of a rose.
Let her ghost dance with the air
let its torch blaze through the streets –

You'd like that, no doubt.
When you've given up running after her
her ghost will issue commands
to do what you've already done.

It's over with you. If she won't feed you
you must stay hungry. She is your guardian
angel, your bodyguard, no one
comes close, you can't love anyone.

Cloud

Nature came to us abhorring sharp edges
raw sunlight and the absence of cloud:

it is November deep in the mist
and by a gate a man stands lost in thought –

how that farm hunkers ruddily in a crease of land
and the dog yaps into the twilight –

We used to say we were walking in the cloud
do you remember? – and we were born there

natives of chrysanthemums, bonfire afternoons,
makers of the finest shades of meaning.

Low over the hill the cloud hangs.
Mist fills the serrations of plough.

I Have Been Thinking of You So Loudly

I have been thinking of you so loudly
that perhaps as you walked down the street you turned
on hearing your name's decibels
sing from pavement, hoardings and walls

until like glass from last night's disasters
your name shattered. Soon sweepers will come
and all my love of you will vanish
as if it had never been.

Meanwhile, hurry before lateness catches you,
run until the wind blows out your coat,
don't stand irresolute
like me, thinking too loudly.

The Kingdom of the Dead

The kingdom of the dead is like an owl
in the heart of the city, hunting
at the Downs' margin.
Over Carter's Steam Fair,
over the illicitly parked cars
where lovers tighten and quicken,
it glides with a tilt of the wing.

The kingdom of the dead is like a mouse
in the owl's eye, a streak of brown
at the Downs' margin.
Under the bright hooves of Carter's horses it hides
this mouse, a drop of water
which flows in its terror
into a beer can.

The kingdom of the dead is like the boot
of a boy in the bliss of fair-time
rucking the grass at the Downs' margin.
Carter's is turning out now, he runs
in and out of the horses
and kicks the beer can
into the touch of heaven.

The Last Heartbeat

The last heartbeat washes the body clean of pain
in a tide of endorphins,
the last sound coils into the ears, and stirs
ossicles, cochlea, the tiny hairs.

For a day or more
long after the onlookers
have turned away
thinking it's all over

the firework show of synapses
and the glorious near-touch
of axons in the brain
slowly dies down
to a last, exquisite connection.

The Old Mastery

Weary and longing to go home
you dress slowly.
Not much of your wardrobe likes you.

You reach for those trousers again
and buff up your shoes
with the old mastery.

The Overcoat

It wears a smell of earth, not air.
I am under it forever.
Sometimes I sleep, sometimes I shiver.

There is a map and I am on it.
the bed's icy geography
is iron, dust-devil, ticking.

Sometimes I fetch from my dreams
the shapes of neighbours, friends,
the smell of rubber perishing.

Sometimes the bed-springs groan
under the weight of the coat.
It will not let me out.

I hold fear so steadily
it stays all in one piece.
I hold the coat's collar.

I hold my breath while the ghost
that lives inside it slides past me
and is bequeathed.

Window Cleaners at Ladysmith Road

Some swear by vinegar and some by newspaper.
Some brandish a shammy leather.

Here they come with their creamy forearms,
their raw red hands, pinnies and aprons
until they stand at my shoulder.

I smell them but don't dare turn.
They are judging smears on the glass,
and as for me and the present
they'll soon have that off.

A warped shine shows the street buckling
into the past, as helpless as I am
not to reflect those boys on the corner
smoking Woodbines from the tobacconist's
which no longer exists.

I Heard You Sing in the Dark

(for Tess)

I heard you sing in the dark
a few clear notes on the stairs

a blackbird in the cold of dusk
forever folding your wings

and slipping, rustling down
past leaves and ivy knots

to where your song bubbled
out of the crevices
into cold, clear February dusk.

I heard the notes plain
rising to the surface
of evening and then down again

almost chuckling, in a blackbird's cold
liquid delight, and so I turned
on the landing, and you were gone.

La Recouvrance

The schooner *La Recouvrance* is almost at the horizon now, sailing south-west. Much closer, the sea is recovering ground. In town the equinoctial spring tides will bring water up the slipway, over the wall and into the sandbagged streets. But here the tide can rise as far as it likes. This cove will be swallowed up soon. Anyone foolish enough to wait too long before they climb the rocks will be washed away like their own footprints. Each small, collapsing wave darkens another arc of the white sand. If you watch it like this you'll be entranced and you won't move until it's too late. Today the sea has a particular smell that isn't like sea at all. If you had your eyes closed you would guess at flowers in the distance. Nothing sweet or perfumed, but a sharp, early narcissus.

You've brought the child down here with you, although it's not very safe. You lift her over the clefts and gullies, carrying everything you need in a back-pack and coming back for her. She waits for you obediently, perched above the drop.

There are just the two of you in the sea. Thigh deep, and now waist deep. The incoming tide pushes against you, and you hold the child's hand, but there are no rips here. Every so often a wave lifts her off her feet. She can swim quite strongly now, and the lift of the sea makes her laugh, showing her sharp little teeth. She dips her head under a wave and brings it up. Her long hair is plastered to her skull and water streams down her face, shining.

You say it's time to go now. She swims into your arms and her strong, cold little body clings to yours. She winds her legs around your waist. Together you stagger towards the shore, but while you are still in the sea's embrace you turn back to see *La Recouvrance* one last time. Her tall masts have vanished. Already she has dipped below the horizon, as she sails away to the bottom of the world.

The Filament

Step by step, holding the thread,
step by step into the dark,

step by step, holding a flag of light
where the tunnel in secrecy closes
like fist or crocus.

My footsteps follow your footsteps
into the dark where they are still
after all these years
just beyond my hearing,

so I call to you in the language
that even now we speak
because you taught me to be haunted
by the catch and space of it –
because we paid for it.

At the tunnel's end a black lake,
a small, desultory boat,
the pluck of the water
as the boat shapes from the shore
while a boatman reads his newspaper
with a desultory air.

The cave roof glistens.
The ribs and flanks of the chamber
all give back the dark water.
I am ready for the journey –
Shall we take ship together? –

Shall we lift my torch into the boat
and sit athwart?
Shall we pass our hands quickly
through crocus and saffron

like children playing with matches?
Even if the boat never sets sail
we can be content,

and I won't look at your face
or write another word.